Collins First French Picture Dictionary

14

Written by Christine Mabileau and Irene Yates
Illustrated by Nick Sharratt
Consultant Editor: Ginny Lapage

Collins

Managing Editor: Jilly MacLeod
Art Director: Rachel Hamdi
Design Consultant: Sophie Stericker
Cover Designer: Nicola Croft
Designers: Holly Mann, Sarah Borny

© HarperCollins*Publishers* Ltd 2005

Published by Collins
a division of HarperCollins*Publishers* Ltd
77-85 Fulham Palace Road, London W6 8JB

www.collins.co.uk

Browse the complete Collins Education catalogue at:
www.collinseducation.com

ISBN 0 00 720346 2

Printed in Thailand by Imago

Contents

How to use
this book   4

Fun and games
at home   6

Look at me!   8

Come to my
birthday party   10

Having fun at
playschool   12

What do we like
to wear?   14

Let's play in
the garden   16

Take a walk down
our street   18

Things that go   20

Let's go to
the toy shop   22

At the supermarket   24

Food to help
me grow   26

Take me to
the pet shop   28

What's in the park   30

Big beasts and
minibeasts   32

Down on the farm   34

A sunny day at
the seaside   36

See what we
can do!   38

Colours are
everywhere   40

Come and count
with me   42

All year round   44

Index   46

How to use this book

Children love playing with words, and learning a new language can be lots of fun. This colourful dictionary is specially designed to help you introduce your child to French. With your help, your child will learn key words from a range of familiar situations, discovering new sounds along the way. They will also start to recognize some of the differences and similarities between French and English.

First steps to learning French

As soon as they are comfortable expressing themselves in their own language, children are ready to learn a new one. To get the best out of this book, sit with your child and encourage them to look at the pictures, to say the French words as often as possible,

Tom

Elisha

Jake

Read the heading out loud so your child knows the context of the French words.

Point to the picture, then run your finger along the French words, from left to right, saying the words out loud. Ask you child to repeat the words, not forgetting to say the short word in front.

Compare the French word with the English, pointing out the similarities as well as the differences between the two languages.

Look for me on every page – sometimes you will have to look very hard! It's fun to see what I'm doing.

Having fun at playschool

l'ordinateur
computer

la maîtresse
teacher

le livre
book

les ciseaux
scissors

la peinture
paint

le pinceau
paintbrush

les crayons
crayons

la colle
glue

and to answer all the questions. Come back to the book time and time again, so your child absorbs the new sounds and learns to associate the French words with the pictures.

Questions and answers

Nick Sharrat's lively scenes will help your child to memorize the French words by putting them into context. They also offer plenty of scope for further questions, so you can encourage your child to practice speaking their newly learned words. For your own guidance, there is a pronunciation guide at the back of the book.

Ask the questions, encouraging your child always to answer in French. (The answers will be words featured on the spread.)

Encourage your child to point out and name real objects around them whenever possible.

Make up your own questions, based on what's going on in the picture. Once your child has learned about colours and numbers (see pages 40-43), you can incorporate these in your questions too, for example, "How many paintbrushes can you count?"

Learning the names of the characters will add to the fun your child gets from using this book.

Ask your child to match objects in the main picture with those shown on the left, and vice versa. When looking for an object, encourage your child always to use its French name.

Lucy

Taz

Amy

Fun and games at home

la porte
door

la fenêtre
window

la chaise
chair

le canapé
sofa

le coussin
cushion

la pendule
clock

la télévision
television

le téléphone
telephone

la tête
head

les cheveux
hair

le visage
face

le nez
nose

les yeux
eyes

les oreilles
ears

les dents
teeth

la bouche
mouth

le cou
neck

l'épaule
shoulder

What do you smell things with?

Come to my birthday party

le ballon
balloon

le masque
mask

le cadeau
present

le chapeau en papier
party hat

la glace
ice cream

le gâteau
cake

le jus de fruit
fruit juice

les bonbons
sweets

l'ordinateur
computer

la maîtresse
teacher

le livre
book

les ciseaux
scissors

la peinture
paint

le pinceau
paintbrush

la colle
glue

les crayons
crayons

12

la veste
jacket

la chemise
shirt

le pantalon
trousers

la jupe
skirt

la robe
dress

le short
shorts

les chaussettes
socks

les chaussures
shoes

What do you like to wear best?

What do you wear on your hands?

le pyjama
pyjamas

la chemise de nuit
nightie

le caleçon
pants

la culotte
knickers

le pull
jumper

le T-shirt
T-shirt

le bonnet
hat

les gants
gloves

Let's play in the garden

la tondeuse
lawnmower

la brouette
wheelbarrow

le papillon
butterfly

l'oiseau
bird

l'arrosoir
watering can

le vélo
bike

la pataugeoire
paddling pool

la fleur
flower

Take a walk down our street

la maison
house

la voiture
car

le magasin
shop

le lampadaire
street light

le fauteuil roulant
wheelchair

l'agent de police
policeman

les feux
traffic light

la route
road

Where do you go to buy things?

18

Things that go

les rollers
rollerblades

le camion
lorry

le bus
bus

la moto
motorbike

l'excavateur
digger

le camion benne
dumper truck

le bateau
boat

le skateboard
skateboard

Let's go to the toy shop

le puzzle
jigsaw puzzle

le camion
truck

le garage
garage

la maison de poupées
doll's house

l'ours en peluche
teddy bear

la poupée
doll

la marionnette
puppet

les cubes
blocks

le bocal
jar

le sac
bag

la boîte de conserve
tin

le panier
basket

le caddy
trolley

l'argent
money

la caisse
checkout

la bouteille
bottle

Food to help me grow

les fruits
fruit

les légumes
vegetables

le riz
rice

le hamburger
hamburger

les frites
chips

les spaghetti
spaghetti

les céréales
cereal

What do you
eat for breakfast?

26

Take me to the pet shop

le lapin
rabbit

le hamster
hamster

le chaton
kitten

le chiot
puppy

le poisson rouge
goldfish

le panier
basket

la cage
cage

la perruche
budgie

le toboggan
slide

la balançoire
swing

la poussette
buggy

la cage à grimper
climbing frame

le banc
bench

l'arbre
tree

le chien
dog

le canard
duck

Big beasts and minibeasts

le kangourou
kangaroo

le lion
lion

la girafe
giraffe

le panda
panda

l'éléphant
elephant

le crocodile
crocodile

la baleine
whale

Down on the farm

Le fermier
farmer

le tracteur
tractor

la poule
hen

l'agneau
lamb

le cheval
horse

la vache
cow

la barrière
gate

le foin
hay

34

le coquillage
shell

le crabe
crab

la mouette
seagull

le château de sable
sand castle

le ballon de plage
beach ball

la vague
wave

le seau
bucket

la pelle
spade

See what we can do!

il saute
he jumps

il marche
he walks

elle court
she runs

elle applaudit
she claps

elle porte
she carries

What is the girl with the box doing?

il peint
he paints

ils dansent they dance

Colours are everywhere

violet
purple

rouge
red

noir
black

bleu
blue

jaune
yellow

What colour is the bouncy castle?

1 un

How many windows does this house have?

2 deux

3 trois

4 quatre

5 cinq

Count the spots on the ladybird.

6 six

7 Sept

8 huit

9 neuf

10 dix

lundi
Monday

mardi
Tuesday

mercredi
Wednesday

jeudi
Thursday

vendredi
Friday

samedi
Saturday

dimanche
Sunday

le jour
day

la nuit
night

What day of the week is it?

What makes you put up your umbrella?

le soleil
sun

la pluie
rain

le vent
wind

la neige
snow

How the words sound

A

aeroplane	l'avion – *lavy**on***
ambulance	l'ambulance – *l**an**bul**ans***
arm	le bras – *le bra*

B

bag	le sac – *le sak*
balloon	le ballon – *le bal**on***
basket	le panier – *le panyay*
beach ball	le ballon de plage – *le bal**on** de pla**j***
bee	l'abeille – *labay*
beetle	le scarabée – *le scarabay*
bench	le banc – *le ban*
bike	le vélo – *le vaylo*
bird	l' oiseau – *lwazo*
biscuits	les biscuits – *lay beeskwee*
black	noir – *nwar*
blocks	les cubes – *lay k**ub***
blue	bleu – *bl**e***
boat	le bateau – *le bato*
book	le livre – *le leevr*
bottle	la bouteille – *la bootay*
bottom	le derrière – *le deryayr*
bread	le pain – *le p**in***
brown	marron – *mar**on***
brushes, she	elle brosse – *el bros*

bucket	le seau – *le so*
budgie	la perruche – *la per**ush***
buggy	la poussette – *la poosset*
bus	le bus – *le b**us***
butterfly	le papillon – *le papeey**on***

C

cage	la cage – *la ka**j***
cake	le gâteau – *le gato*
car	la voiture – *la vwat**ur***
carries, she	elle porte – *el port*
caterpillar	la chenille – *la sheneey*
cereal	les céréales – *lay sayrayhal*
chair	la chaise – *la shez*
checkout	la caisse – *la kess*
cheese	le fromage – *le froma**j***
chicken	le poulet – *le poolay*
chips	les frites – *lay freet*
claps, she	elle applaudit – *el aplodee*
climbing frame	la cage à grimper – *la ka**j** a gr**in**pay*
clock	la pendule – *la p**an**d**ul***
computer	l'ordinateur – *l'ordinat**er***
cow	la vache – *la vash*
crab	le crabe – *le krab*
cries, he	il pleure – *eel pler*
crocodile	le crocodile – *le krokodeel*
cushion	le coussin – *le koos**sin***
cuts, she	elle coupe – *el koop*

D

dance, they	ils dansent – *eel d**ans***
day	le jour – *le joor*
digger	l'excavateur – *lexkavat**er***
dog	le chien – *le shee**in***
doll	la poupée – *la poopay*
dolls house	la maison de poupées – *la mayzon d**e** poopay*
door	la porte – *la port*
dress	la robe – *la rob*
drinks, she	elle boit – *el bwa*
duck	le canard – *le kanar*
dumper truck	le camion benne – *le kamy**on** ben*

E

ears	les oreilles – *lay zoray*
eats, she	elle mange – *el manj*
eggs	les œufs – *lay ze*
eight	huit – *weet*
elbow	le coude – *le kood*
elephant	l'éléphant – *lelefan*
eyes	les yeux – *layzye*

F

face	le visage – *le veezaj*
farmer	le fermier – *le fayrmyay*
finger	le doigt – *le dwa*
fire engine	le camion de pompiers – *le kamyon de ponpyay*
fish	le poisson – *le pwasson*
five	cinq – *sink*
flower	la fleur – *la fler*
fly	la mouche – *la moosh*
foot	le pied – *le pyay*
four	quatre – *katr*
Friday	vendredi – *vandredee*
fruit	les fruits – *lay frwee*
fruit juice	le jus de fruit – *le ju de frwee*

G

garage	le garage – *le garaj*
gate	la barrière – *la baryayr*
giraffe	la girafe – *la jeeraf*
gloves	les gants – *lay gan*
glue	la colle – *la kol*
goldfish	le poisson rouge – *le pwasson rooj*
green	vert – *vayr*

H

hair	les cheveux – *lay sheve*
hamburger	le hamburger – *le hamburger*
hamster	le hamster – *le amster*
hand	la main – *la min*
hat	le bonnet – *le bonay*
hay	le foin – *le fwin*
head	la tête – *la tet*
helicopter	l'hélicoptère – *lelikoptayr*
hen	la poule – *la pool*
horse	le cheval – *le sheval*
hot air balloon	la montgolfière – *la mongolfyear*
house	la maison – *la mayzon*

I J

ice cream	la glace – *la glass*
jacket	la veste – *la vest*
jar	le bocal – *le bokal*
jigsaw puzzle	le puzzle – *le puzl*
jumps, he	il saute – *eel sot*
jumper	le pull – *le pul*

K

kangaroo	le kangourou – *le kangooroo*
kitten	le chaton – *le shaton*
knee	le genou – *le jenoo*
knickers	la culotte – *la kulot*

L

ladybird	la coccinnelle – *la cokseenel*
lamb	l'agneau – *lanyo*
laughs, he	il rit – *eel ree*
lawnmower	la tondeuse – *la tonderz*
leg	la jambe – *la janb*
lion	le lion – *le lyon*
lorry	le camion – *le kamyon*

M

mask	le masque – *le mask*
milk	le lait – *le lay*
Monday	lundi – *landee*
money	l'argent – *larjan*
motor bike	la moto – *la moto*
mouth	la bouche – *la bush*

N

night	la nuit – *la nwee*
night-dress	la chemise de nuit – *la shemeez de nwee*
nine	neuf – *nerf*
nose	le nez – *le nay*
neck	le cou – *le koo*

O

one	un – *an*
orange	orange – *oranj*

P

paddling pool	la pataugeoire – *la patojwar*
paints, he	il peint – *eel pin*
paintbrush	le pinceau – *le pinso*
panda	le panda – *le panda*
pants	le caleçon – *le kalson*
party hat	le chapeau en papier – *le shapo an papyay*
pen	les crayons – *lay krayon*
pink	rose – *rose*
pizza	la pizza – *la peedza*
policeman	l'agent de police – *lajan de police*
present	le cadeau – *le kado*
puppet	la marionnette – *la maryonet*
puppy	le chiot – *le shyo*
purple	violet – *vyolay*
pyjamas	le pyjama – *le peejama*

R

rabbit	le lapin – *le lapin*
rain	la pluie – *la plwee*
red	rouge – *rooj*
rice	le riz – *le ree*
road	la route – *la root*
rocket	la fusée – *la fuzay*
rollerblades	les rollers – *lay roller*
runs, she	elle court – *el koor*

S

sandcastle	le château de sable – *le shato de sable*
Saturday	samedi – *samedee*
scissors	les ciseaux – *lay seezo*
seagull	la mouette – *la mwet*
seven	Sept – *set*
shell	le coquillage – *le kokeeyaj*
shirt	la chemise – *la shemeez*
shoes	les chaussures – *lay shossur*
shop	le magasin – *le magazin*
shorts	le short – *le short*
shoulder	l'épaule – *laypol*
sings, he	il chante – *eel shant*
six	six – *seess*
skateboard	le skateboard – *le skateboard*
skirt	la jupe – *la jup*
slide	le toboggan – *le tobogan*
snail	l'escargot – *leskargo*
snow	la neige – *la nej*
socks	les chaussettes – *lay shosset*
sofa	le canapé – *le kanapay*

spade	la pelle – *la pel*
spaghetti	les spaghetti – *lay spaghetti*
spider	l'araignée – *laraynyay*
street light	le lampadaire – *le lanpadayr*
sun	le soleil – *le soley*
Sunday	dimanche – *deemansh*
sweets	les bonbons – *lay bonbon*
swing	la balançoire – *la balanswar*

T

teacher	la maîtresse – *la maytrayss*
teddy bear	l'ours en peluche – *loors an pelush*
teeth	les dents – *lay dan*
telephone	le téléphone – *le telefon*
television	la télévision – *la televeezyon*
ten	dix – *deess*
three	trois – *trwa*
thumb	le pouce – *le pooss*
Thursday	jeudi – *jedee*
tin	la boîte de conserve – *la bwat de konserv*
toe	l'orteil – *lortay*
tractor	le tracteur – *le trakter*
traffic light	les feux – *lay fe*
train	le train – *le trin*
tree	l'arbre – *larbr*
trolley	le caddy – *le kadee*
trousers	le pantalon – *le pantalon*
truck	le camion – *le kamyon*
T-shirt	le T-shirt – *le tee-shirt*
Tuesday	mardi – *mardee*
tummy	le ventre – *le vantr*
two	deux – *de*

U V W

vegetables	les légumes – *lay laygum*
walks, he	il marche – *eel marsh*
watering can	l'arrosoir – *larozwar*
wave	la vague – *la vague*
Wednesday	mercredi – *mayrcredee*
whale	la baleine – *la balen*
wheelbarrow	la brouette – *la broohet*
wheelchair	le fauteuil roulant – *le fotey roolan*
white	blanc – *blan*
wind	le vent – *le van*
window	la fenêtre – *la fenetr*
worm	le ver de terre – *le vayr de tayr*

X Y Z

yellow	jaune – *jon*
yoghurt	le yaourt – *le yahoort*